ONE LINE
A DAY

A SIX-YEAR MEMORY BOOK

WE DO NOT
REMEMBER DAYS; WE
REMEMBER
MOMENTS. - CESARE
PAVESE

GOALS FOR JANUARY

20_ 1. _____

2. _____

20_ 1. _____

2. _____

20_ 1. _____

2. _____

20_ 1. _____

2. _____

20_ 1. _____

2. _____

20_ 1. _____

2. _____

JANUARY 1

20__ _____
_____
_____

20__ _____
_____
_____

20__ _____
_____
_____

20__ _____
_____
_____

20__ _____
_____
_____

20__ _____
_____
_____

JANUARY 2

20___ _____

_____

_____

20___ _____

_____

_____

20___ _____

_____

_____

20___ _____

_____

_____

20___ _____

_____

_____

20___ _____

_____

_____

JANUARY 3

20___ _____

_____

_____

20___ _____

_____

_____

20___ _____

_____

_____

20___ _____

_____

_____

20___ _____

_____

_____

20___ _____

_____

_____

JANUARY 4

20__ _____

_____

_____

20__ _____

_____

_____

20__ _____

_____

_____

20__ _____

_____

_____

20__ _____

_____

_____

20__ _____

_____

_____

JANUARY 5

20__ _____

_____

20__ _____

_____

20__ _____

_____

20__ _____

_____

20__ _____

_____

20__ _____

_____

JANUARY 6

20__ _____

_____

_____

20__ _____

_____

_____

20__ _____

_____

_____

20__ _____

_____

_____

20__ _____

_____

_____

20__ _____

_____

_____

JANUARY 7

20__ _____

_____

_____

20__ _____

_____

_____

20__ _____

_____

_____

20__ _____

_____

_____

20__ _____

_____

_____

20__ _____

_____

_____

JANUARY 8

20__ _____

_____

_____

20__ _____

_____

_____

20__ _____

_____

_____

20__ _____

_____

_____

20__ _____

_____

_____

20__ _____

_____

_____

JANUARY 9

20__ _____

_____

20__ _____

_____

20__ _____

_____

20__ _____

_____

20__ _____

_____

20__ _____

_____

JANUARY 10

20__ _____

_____

_____

20__ _____

_____

_____

20__ _____

_____

_____

20__ _____

_____

_____

20__ _____

_____

_____

20__ _____

_____

_____

JANUARY 11

20__ _____

_____

_____

20__ _____

_____

_____

20__ _____

_____

_____

20__ _____

_____

_____

20__ _____

_____

_____

20__ _____

_____

_____

JANUARY 12

20__ _____

_____

_____

20__ _____

_____

_____

20__ _____

_____

_____

20__ _____

_____

_____

20__ _____

_____

_____

20__ _____

_____

_____

JANUARY 13

20__ _____

_____

_____

20__ _____

_____

_____

20__ _____

_____

_____

20__ _____

_____

_____

20__ _____

_____

_____

20__ _____

_____

_____

JANUARY 14

20___ _____

_____

_____

20___ _____

_____

_____

20___ _____

_____

_____

20___ _____

_____

_____

20___ _____

_____

_____

20___ _____

_____

_____

JANUARY 15

20__ _____

_____

_____

20__ _____

_____

_____

20__ _____

_____

_____

20__ _____

_____

_____

20__ _____

_____

_____

20__ _____

_____

_____

JANUARY 16

20__ _____

_____

_____

20__ _____

_____

_____

20__ _____

_____

_____

20__ _____

_____

_____

20__ _____

_____

_____

20__ _____

_____

_____

JANUARY 17

20__ _____

_____

_____

20__ _____

_____

_____

20__ _____

_____

_____

20__ _____

_____

_____

20__ _____

_____

_____

20__ _____

_____

_____

JANUARY 18

20___ _____

_____

_____

20___ _____

_____

_____

20___ _____

_____

_____

20___ _____

_____

_____

20___ _____

_____

_____

20___ _____

_____

_____

JANUARY 19

20__ _____

_____

_____

20__ _____

_____

_____

20__ _____

_____

_____

20__ _____

_____

_____

20__ _____

_____

_____

20__ _____

_____

_____

JANUARY 20

20__ _____

_____

_____

20__ _____

_____

_____

20__ _____

_____

_____

20__ _____

_____

_____

20__ _____

_____

_____

20__ _____

_____

_____

JANUARY 21

20__ _____

_____

_____

20__ _____

_____

_____

20__ _____

_____

_____

20__ _____

_____

_____

20__ _____

_____

_____

20__ _____

_____

_____

JANUARY 22

20__ _____

_____

_____

20__ _____

_____

_____

20__ _____

_____

_____

20__ _____

_____

_____

20__ _____

_____

_____

20__ _____

_____

_____

JANUARY 23

20__ _____

_____

_____

20__ _____

_____

_____

20__ _____

_____

_____

20__ _____

_____

_____

20__ _____

_____

_____

20__ _____

_____

_____

JANUARY 24

20___ _____

_____

_____

20___ _____

_____

_____

20___ _____

_____

_____

20___ _____

_____

_____

20___ _____

_____

_____

20___ _____

_____

_____

JANUARY 25

20__ _____

_____

_____

20__ _____

_____

_____

20__ _____

_____

_____

20__ _____

_____

_____

20__ _____

_____

_____

20__ _____

_____

_____

JANUARY 26

20__ _____

_____

_____

20__ _____

_____

_____

20__ _____

_____

_____

20__ _____

_____

_____

20__ _____

_____

_____

20__ _____

_____

_____

JANUARY 27

20__ _____

_____

_____

20__ _____

_____

_____

20__ _____

_____

_____

20__ _____

_____

_____

20__ _____

_____

_____

20__ _____

_____

_____

JANUARY 28

20__ _____

_____

_____

20__ _____

_____

_____

20__ _____

_____

_____

20__ _____

_____

_____

20__ _____

_____

_____

20__ _____

_____

_____

JANUARY 29

20__ _____

_____

_____

20__ _____

_____

_____

20__ _____

_____

_____

20__ _____

_____

_____

20__ _____

_____

_____

20__ _____

_____

_____

JANUARY 30

20___ _____

_____

_____

20___ _____

_____

_____

20___ _____

_____

_____

20___ _____

_____

_____

20___ _____

_____

_____

20___ _____

_____

_____

JANUARY 31

20__ _____

_____

_____

20__ _____

_____

_____

20__ _____

_____

_____

20__ _____

_____

_____

20__ _____

_____

_____

20__ _____

_____

_____

DATES TO REMEMBER

GOALS FOR FEBRUARY

20_ 1. _____

2. _____

20_ 1. _____

2. _____

20_ 1. _____

2. _____

20_ 1. _____

2. _____

20_ 1. _____

2. _____

20_ 1. _____

2. _____

FEBRUARY 1

20__ _____
_____

20__ _____
_____

20__ _____
_____

20__ _____
_____

20__ _____
_____

20__ _____
_____

FEBRUARY 2

20__ _____

_____

_____

20__ _____

_____

_____

20__ _____

_____

_____

20__ _____

_____

_____

20__ _____

_____

_____

20__ _____

_____

_____

FEBRUARY 3

20___ _____

_____

20___ _____

_____

20___ _____

_____

20___ _____

_____

20___ _____

_____

20___ _____

_____

FEBRUARY 4

20___ _____

_____

_____

20___ _____

_____

_____

20___ _____

_____

_____

20___ _____

_____

_____

20___ _____

_____

_____

20___ _____

_____

_____

FEBRUARY 5

20__ _____

_____

20__ _____

_____

20__ _____

_____

20__ _____

_____

20__ _____

_____

20__ _____

_____

FEBRUARY 6

20___ _____

_____

_____

20___ _____

_____

_____

20___ _____

_____

_____

20___ _____

_____

_____

20___ _____

_____

_____

20___ _____

_____

_____

FEBRUARY 7

20__ _____

_____

_____

20__ _____

_____

_____

20__ _____

_____

_____

20__ _____

_____

_____

20__ _____

_____

_____

20__ _____

_____

_____

FEBRUARY 8

20__ _____

_____

_____

20__ _____

_____

_____

20__ _____

_____

_____

20__ _____

_____

_____

20__ _____

_____

_____

20__ _____

_____

_____

FEBRUARY 9

20__ _____

_____

_____

20__ _____

_____

_____

20__ _____

_____

_____

20__ _____

_____

_____

20__ _____

_____

_____

20__ _____

_____

_____

FEBRUARY 10

20__ _____

_____

_____

20__ _____

_____

_____

20__ _____

_____

_____

20__ _____

_____

_____

20__ _____

_____

_____

20__ _____

_____

_____

FEBRUARY 11

20__ _____

_____

_____

20__ _____

_____

_____

20__ _____

_____

_____

20__ _____

_____

_____

20__ _____

_____

_____

20__ _____

_____

_____

FEBRUARY 12

20__ _____

_____

_____

20__ _____

_____

_____

20__ _____

_____

_____

20__ _____

_____

_____

20__ _____

_____

_____

20__ _____

_____

_____

FEBRUARY 13

20___ _____

_____

_____

20___ _____

_____

_____

20___ _____

_____

_____

20___ _____

_____

_____

20___ _____

_____

_____

20___ _____

_____

_____

FEBRUARY 14

20__ _____

_____

_____

20__ _____

_____

_____

20__ _____

_____

_____

20__ _____

_____

_____

20__ _____

_____

_____

20__ _____

_____

_____

FEBRUARY 15

20__ _____

_____

20__ _____

_____

20__ _____

_____

20__ _____

_____

20__ _____

_____

20__ _____

_____

FEBRUARY 16

20___ _____

_____

_____

20___ _____

_____

_____

20___ _____

_____

_____

20___ _____

_____

_____

20___ _____

_____

_____

20___ _____

_____

_____

FEBRUARY 17

20___ _____

_____

_____

20___ _____

_____

_____

20___ _____

_____

_____

20___ _____

_____

_____

20___ _____

_____

_____

20___ _____

_____

_____

FEBRUARY 18

20__ _____

_____

20__ _____

_____

20__ _____

_____

20__ _____

_____

20__ _____

_____

20__ _____

_____

FEBRUARY 19

20__ _____

_____

_____

20__ _____

_____

_____

20__ _____

_____

_____

20__ _____

_____

_____

20__ _____

_____

_____

20__ _____

_____

_____

FEBRUARY 20

20__ _____

_____

20__ _____

_____

20__ _____

_____

20__ _____

_____

20__ _____

_____

20__ _____

_____

FEBRUARY 21

20___ _____

_____

_____

20___ _____

_____

_____

20___ _____

_____

_____

20___ _____

_____

_____

20___ _____

_____

_____

20___ _____

_____

_____

FEBRUARY 22

20___ _____

_____

_____

20___ _____

_____

_____

20___ _____

_____

_____

20___ _____

_____

_____

20___ _____

_____

_____

20___ _____

_____

_____

FEBRUARY 23

20__ _____

_____

20__ _____

_____

20__ _____

_____

20__ _____

_____

20__ _____

_____

20__ _____

_____

FEBRUARY 24

20__ ----------------------------

_____

20__ ----------------------------

_____

20__ ----------------------------

_____

20__ ----------------------------

_____

20__ ----------------------------

_____

20__ ----------------------------

_____

FEBRUARY 25

20__ _____

_____

_____

20__ _____

_____

_____

20__ _____

_____

_____

20__ _____

_____

_____

20__ _____

_____

_____

20__ _____

_____

_____

FEBRUARY 26

20__ _____

_____

_____

20__ _____

_____

_____

20__ _____

_____

_____

20__ _____

_____

_____

20__ _____

_____

_____

20__ _____

_____

_____

FEBRUARY 27

20__ _____

_____

20__ _____

_____

20__ _____

_____

20__ _____

_____

20__ _____

_____

20__ _____

_____

FEBRUARY 28

20__ _____

_____

_____

20__ _____

_____

_____

20__ _____

_____

_____

20__ _____

_____

_____

20__ _____

_____

_____

20__ _____

_____

_____

DATES TO REMEMBER

GOALS FOR MARCH

20_ 1. _____

2. _____

20_ 1. _____

2. _____

20_ 1. _____

2. _____

20_ 1. _____

2. _____

20_ 1. _____

2. _____

20_ 1. _____

2. _____

MARCH 1

20__ _____

_____

_____

20__ _____

_____

_____

20__ _____

_____

_____

20__ _____

_____

_____

20__ _____

_____

_____

20__ _____

_____

_____

MARCH 2

20__ _____

_____

_____

20__ _____

_____

_____

20__ _____

_____

_____

20__ _____

_____

_____

20__ _____

_____

_____

20__ _____

_____

_____

MARCH 3

20___ _____
_____
_____

20___ _____
_____
_____

20___ _____
_____
_____

20___ _____
_____
_____

20___ _____
_____
_____

20___ _____
_____
_____

MARCH 4

20__ _____

_____

_____

20__ _____

_____

_____

20__ _____

_____

_____

20__ _____

_____

_____

20__ _____

_____

_____

20__ _____

_____

_____

MARCH 5

20__ _____
_____
_____

20__ _____
_____
_____

20__ _____
_____
_____

20__ _____
_____
_____

20__ _____
_____
_____

20__ _____
_____
_____

MARCH 6

20__ _____

_____

_____

20__ _____

_____

_____

20__ _____

_____

_____

20__ _____

_____

_____

20__ _____

_____

_____

20__ _____

_____

_____

MARCH 7

20__ _____

_____

_____

20__ _____

_____

_____

20__ _____

_____

_____

20__ _____

_____

_____

20__ _____

_____

_____

20__ _____

_____

_____

MARCH 8

20__ _____

_____

_____

20__ _____

_____

_____

20__ _____

_____

_____

20__ _____

_____

_____

20__ _____

_____

_____

20__ _____

_____

_____

MARCH 9

20___ _____

_____

20___ _____

_____

20___ _____

_____

20___ _____

_____

20___ _____

_____

20___ _____

_____

MARCH 10

20__ _____

_____

_____

20__ _____

_____

_____

20__ _____

_____

_____

20__ _____

_____

_____

20__ _____

_____

_____

20__ _____

_____

_____

MARCH 11

20___ _____

_____

20___ _____

_____

20___ _____

_____

20___ _____

_____

20___ _____

_____

20___ _____

_____

MARCH 12

20__ _____

_____

_____

20__ _____

_____

_____

20__ _____

_____

_____

20__ _____

_____

_____

20__ _____

_____

_____

20__ _____

_____

_____

MARCH 13

20__ _____

_____

_____

20__ _____

_____

_____

20__ _____

_____

_____

20__ _____

_____

_____

20__ _____

_____

_____

20__ _____

_____

_____

MARCH 14

20___ _____

_____

_____

20___ _____

_____

_____

20___ _____

_____

_____

20___ _____

_____

_____

20___ _____

_____

_____

20___ _____

_____

_____

MARCH 15

20__ _____

_____

_____

20__ _____

_____

_____

20__ _____

_____

_____

20__ _____

_____

_____

20__ _____

_____

_____

20__ _____

_____

_____

MARCH 16

20__ _____

_____

_____

20__ _____

_____

_____

20__ _____

_____

_____

20__ _____

_____

_____

20__ _____

_____

_____

20__ _____

_____

_____

MARCH 17

20__ _____

_____

_____

20__ _____

_____

_____

20__ _____

_____

_____

20__ _____

_____

_____

20__ _____

_____

_____

20__ _____

_____

_____

MARCH 18

20__ _____

_____

_____

20__ _____

_____

_____

20__ _____

_____

_____

20__ _____

_____

_____

20__ _____

_____

_____

20__ _____

_____

_____

MARCH 19

20__ _____

_____

20__ _____

_____

20__ _____

_____

20__ _____

_____

20__ _____

_____

20__ _____

_____

MARCH 20

20__ _____

_____

_____

20__ _____

_____

_____

20__ _____

_____

_____

20__ _____

_____

_____

20__ _____

_____

_____

20__ _____

_____

_____

MARCH 21

20___ _____

_____

_____

20___ _____

_____

_____

20___ _____

_____

_____

20___ _____

_____

_____

20___ _____

_____

_____

20___ _____

_____

_____

MARCH 22

20___ _____

_____

_____

20___ _____

_____

_____

20___ _____

_____

_____

20___ _____

_____

_____

20___ _____

_____

_____

20___ _____

_____

_____

MARCH 23

20__ _____

_____

_____

20__ _____

_____

_____

20__ _____

_____

_____

20__ _____

_____

_____

20__ _____

_____

_____

20__ _____

_____

_____

MARCH 24

20__ _____

_____

20__ _____

_____

20__ _____

_____

20__ _____

_____

20__ _____

_____

20__ _____

_____

MARCH 25

20____ _____

_____

_____

20____ _____

_____

_____

20____ _____

_____

_____

20____ _____

_____

_____

20____ _____

_____

_____

20____ _____

_____

_____

MARCH 26

20__ _____

_____

_____

20__ _____

_____

_____

20__ _____

_____

_____

20__ _____

_____

_____

20__ _____

_____

_____

20__ _____

_____

_____

MARCH 27

20__ _____
_____
_____

20__ _____
_____
_____

20__ _____
_____
_____

20__ _____
_____
_____

20__ _____
_____
_____

20__ _____
_____
_____

MARCH 28

20__ _____

_____

_____

20__ _____

_____

_____

20__ _____

_____

_____

20__ _____

_____

_____

20__ _____

_____

_____

20__ _____

_____

_____

MARCH 29

20__ _____

_____

_____

20__ _____

_____

_____

20__ _____

_____

_____

20__ _____

_____

_____

20__ _____

_____

_____

20__ _____

_____

_____

MARCH 30

20__ _____

_____

_____

20__ _____

_____

_____

20__ _____

_____

_____

20__ _____

_____

_____

20__ _____

_____

_____

20__ _____

_____

_____

MARCH 31

20__ _____

_____

_____

20__ _____

_____

_____

20__ _____

_____

_____

20__ _____

_____

_____

20__ _____

_____

_____

20__ _____

_____

_____

DATES TO REMEMBER

GOALS FOR APRIL

20_ 1. _____

2. _____

20_ 1. _____

2. _____

20_ 1. _____

2. _____

20_ 1. _____

2. _____

20_ 1. _____

2. _____

20_ 1. _____

2. _____

APRIL 1

20__ _____

_____

_____

20__ _____

_____

_____

20__ _____

_____

_____

20__ _____

_____

_____

20__ _____

_____

_____

20__ _____

_____

_____

APRIL 2

20___ _____

_____

_____

20___ _____

_____

_____

20___ _____

_____

_____

20___ _____

_____

_____

20___ _____

_____

_____

20___ _____

_____

_____

APRIL 3

20___ _____

_____

_____

20___ _____

_____

_____

20___ _____

_____

_____

20___ _____

_____

_____

20___ _____

_____

_____

20___ _____

_____

_____

APRIL 4

20____ _____

_____

_____

20____ _____

_____

_____

20____ _____

_____

_____

20____ _____

_____

_____

20____ _____

_____

_____

20____ _____

_____

_____

APRIL 5

20__ _____

_____

_____

20__ _____

_____

_____

20__ _____

_____

_____

20__ _____

_____

_____

20__ _____

_____

_____

20__ _____

_____

_____

APRIL 6

20___ _____
_____

20___ _____
_____

20___ _____
_____

20___ _____
_____

20___ _____
_____

20___ _____
_____

APRIL 7

20___ _____

_____

_____

20___ _____

_____

_____

20___ _____

_____

_____

20___ _____

_____

_____

20___ _____

_____

_____

20___ _____

_____

_____

APRIL 8

20__ _____

_____

_____

20__ _____

_____

_____

20__ _____

_____

_____

20__ _____

_____

_____

20__ _____

_____

_____

20__ _____

_____

_____

APRIL 9

20___ _____

_____

_____

20___ _____

_____

_____

20___ _____

_____

_____

20___ _____

_____

_____

20___ _____

_____

_____

20___ _____

_____

_____

APRIL 10

20__ _____

_____

_____

20__ _____

_____

_____

20__ _____

_____

_____

20__ _____

_____

_____

20__ _____

_____

_____

20__ _____

_____

_____

APRIL 11

20__ _____

_____

_____

20__ _____

_____

_____

20__ _____

_____

_____

20__ _____

_____

_____

20__ _____

_____

_____

20__ _____

_____

_____

APRIL 12

20__ _____

_____

_____

20__ _____

_____

_____

20__ _____

_____

_____

20__ _____

_____

_____

20__ _____

_____

_____

20__ _____

_____

_____

APRIL 13

20__ _____

_____

_____

20__ _____

_____

_____

20__ _____

_____

_____

20__ _____

_____

_____

20__ _____

_____

_____

20__ _____

_____

_____

APRIL 14

20__ _____

_____

20__ _____

_____

20__ _____

_____

20__ _____

_____

20__ _____

_____

20__ _____

_____

APRIL 15

20___ _____

_____

_____

20___ _____

_____

_____

20___ _____

_____

_____

20___ _____

_____

_____

20___ _____

_____

_____

20___ _____

_____

_____

APRIL 16

20__ _____

_____

20__ _____

_____

20__ _____

_____

20__ _____

_____

20__ _____

_____

20__ _____

_____

APRIL 17

20__ _____

_____

_____

20__ _____

_____

_____

20__ _____

_____

_____

20__ _____

_____

_____

20__ _____

_____

_____

20__ _____

_____

_____

APRIL 18

20__ _____

_____

20__ _____

_____

20__ _____

_____

20__ _____

_____

20__ _____

_____

20__ _____

_____

APRIL 19

20___ _____

_____

_____

20___ _____

_____

_____

20___ _____

_____

_____

20___ _____

_____

_____

20___ _____

_____

_____

20___ _____

_____

_____

APRIL 20

20__ _____

_____

20__ _____

_____

20__ _____

_____

20__ _____

_____

20__ _____

_____

20__ _____

_____

APRIL 21

20___ _____

_____

_____

20___ _____

_____

_____

20___ _____

_____

_____

20___ _____

_____

_____

20___ _____

_____

_____

20___ _____

_____

_____

APRIL 22

20___ _____

_____

20___ _____

_____

20___ _____

_____

20___ _____

_____

20___ _____

_____

20___ _____

_____

APRIL 23

20__ _____

_____

_____

20__ _____

_____

_____

20__ _____

_____

_____

20__ _____

_____

_____

20__ _____

_____

_____

20__ _____

_____

_____

APRIL 24

20___ _____

_____

20___ _____

_____

20___ _____

_____

20___ _____

_____

20___ _____

_____

20___ _____

_____

APRIL 25

20___ _____

_____

_____

20___ _____

_____

_____

20___ _____

_____

_____

20___ _____

_____

_____

20___ _____

_____

_____

20___ _____

_____

_____

APRIL 26

20___ _____

_____

20___ _____

_____

20___ _____

_____

20___ _____

_____

20___ _____

_____

20___ _____

_____

APRIL 27

20___ _____

_____

_____

20___ _____

_____

_____

20___ _____

_____

_____

20___ _____

_____

_____

20___ _____

_____

_____

20___ _____

_____

_____

APRIL 28

20__ _____

_____

_____

20__ _____

_____

_____

20__ _____

_____

_____

20__ _____

_____

_____

20__ _____

_____

_____

20__ _____

_____

_____

APRIL 29

20__ _____

_____

_____

20__ _____

_____

_____

20__ _____

_____

_____

20__ _____

_____

_____

20__ _____

_____

_____

20__ _____

_____

_____

APRIL 30

20__ _____

_____

_____

20__ _____

_____

_____

20__ _____

_____

_____

20__ _____

_____

_____

20__ _____

_____

_____

20__ _____

_____

_____

DATES TO REMEMBER

GOALS FOR MAY

20_ 1. _____

2. _____

20_ 1. _____

2. _____

20_ 1. _____

2. _____

20_ 1. _____

2. _____

20_ 1. _____

2. _____

20_ 1. _____

2. _____

MAY 1

20___ _____
_____
_____

20___ _____
_____
_____

20___ _____
_____
_____

20___ _____
_____
_____

20___ _____
_____
_____

20___ _____
_____
_____

MAY 2

20___ _____

_____

_____

20___ _____

_____

_____

20___ _____

_____

_____

20___ _____

_____

_____

20___ _____

_____

_____

20___ _____

_____

_____

MAY 3

20__ _____

_____

_____

20__ _____

_____

_____

20__ _____

_____

_____

20__ _____

_____

_____

20__ _____

_____

_____

20__ _____

_____

_____

MAY 4

20___ _____

_____

_____

20___ _____

_____

_____

20___ _____

_____

_____

20___ _____

_____

_____

20___ _____

_____

_____

20___ _____

_____

_____

MAY 5

20___ _____

_____

_____

20___ _____

_____

_____

20___ _____

_____

_____

20___ _____

_____

_____

20___ _____

_____

_____

20___ _____

_____

_____

MAY 6

20___ _____
_____
_____

20___ _____
_____
_____

20___ _____
_____
_____

20___ _____
_____
_____

20___ _____
_____
_____

20___ _____
_____
_____

MAY 7

20__ _____

_____

20__ _____

_____

20__ _____

_____

20__ _____

_____

20__ _____

_____

20__ _____

_____

MAY 8

20__ _____

_____

_____

20__ _____

_____

_____

20__ _____

_____

_____

20__ _____

_____

_____

20__ _____

_____

_____

20__ _____

_____

_____

MAY 9

20__ _____

_____

_____

20__ _____

_____

_____

20__ _____

_____

_____

20__ _____

_____

_____

20__ _____

_____

_____

20__ _____

_____

_____

MAY 10

20__ _____

_____

_____

20__ _____

_____

_____

20__ _____

_____

_____

20__ _____

_____

_____

20__ _____

_____

_____

20__ _____

_____

_____

MAY 11

20__ _____

_____

_____

20__ _____

_____

_____

20__ _____

_____

_____

20__ _____

_____

_____

20__ _____

_____

_____

20__ _____

_____

_____

MAY 12

20__ _____

_____

_____

20__ _____

_____

_____

20__ _____

_____

_____

20__ _____

_____

_____

20__ _____

_____

_____

20__ _____

_____

_____

MAY 13

20__ _____

_____

_____

20__ _____

_____

_____

20__ _____

_____

_____

20__ _____

_____

_____

20__ _____

_____

_____

20__ _____

_____

_____

MAY 14

20__ _____

_____

_____

20__ _____

_____

_____

20__ _____

_____

_____

20__ _____

_____

_____

20__ _____

_____

_____

20__ _____

_____

_____

MAY 15

20__ _____

_____

_____

20__ _____

_____

_____

20__ _____

_____

_____

20__ _____

_____

_____

20__ _____

_____

_____

20__ _____

_____

_____

MAY 16

20__ _____

_____

_____

20__ _____

_____

_____

20__ _____

_____

_____

20__ _____

_____

_____

20__ _____

_____

_____

20__ _____

_____

_____

MAY 17

20__ _____

_____

_____

20__ _____

_____

_____

20__ _____

_____

_____

20__ _____

_____

_____

20__ _____

_____

_____

20__ _____

_____

_____

MAY 18

20__ _____

_____

20__ _____

_____

20__ _____

_____

20__ _____

_____

20__ _____

_____

20__ _____

_____

MAY 19

20__ _____

_____

_____

20__ _____

_____

_____

20__ _____

_____

_____

20__ _____

_____

_____

20__ _____

_____

_____

20__ _____

_____

_____

MAY 20

20__ _____

_____

_____

20__ _____

_____

_____

20__ _____

_____

_____

20__ _____

_____

_____

20__ _____

_____

_____

20__ _____

_____

_____

MAY 21

20__ _____

_____

_____

20__ _____

_____

_____

20__ _____

_____

_____

20__ _____

_____

_____

20__ _____

_____

_____

20__ _____

_____

_____

MAY 22

20___ _____

_____

20___ _____

_____

20___ _____

_____

20___ _____

_____

20___ _____

_____

20___ _____

_____

MAY 23

20__ _____

_____

_____

20__ _____

_____

_____

20__ _____

_____

_____

20__ _____

_____

_____

20__ _____

_____

_____

20__ _____

_____

_____

MAY 24

20__ _____

_____

_____

20__ _____

_____

_____

20__ _____

_____

_____

20__ _____

_____

_____

20__ _____

_____

_____

20__ _____

_____

_____

MAY 25

20__ _____

_____

_____

20__ _____

_____

_____

20__ _____

_____

_____

20__ _____

_____

_____

20__ _____

_____

_____

20__ _____

_____

_____

MAY 26

20___ _____
_____
_____

20___ _____
_____
_____

20___ _____
_____
_____

20___ _____
_____
_____

20___ _____
_____
_____

20___ _____
_____
_____

MAY 27

20____ _____

_____

20____ _____

_____

20____ _____

_____

20____ _____

_____

20____ _____

_____

20____ _____

_____

MAY 28

20___ _____

_____

20___ _____

_____

20___ _____

_____

20___ _____

_____

20___ _____

_____

20___ _____

_____

MAY 29

20__ _____

_____

_____

20__ _____

_____

_____

20__ _____

_____

_____

20__ _____

_____

_____

20__ _____

_____

_____

20__ _____

_____

_____

MAY 30

20___ _____

_____

_____

20___ _____

_____

_____

20___ _____

_____

_____

20___ _____

_____

_____

20___ _____

_____

_____

20___ _____

_____

_____

MAY 31

20__ _____

_____

_____

20__ _____

_____

_____

20__ _____

_____

_____

20__ _____

_____

_____

20__ _____

_____

_____

20__ _____

_____

_____

DATES TO REMEMBER

GOALS FOR JUNE

20_ 1. _____

2. _____

20_ 1. _____

2. _____

20_ 1. _____

2. _____

20_ 1. _____

2. _____

20_ 1. _____

2. _____

20_ 1. _____

2. _____

JUNE 1

20__ _____
_____
_____

20__ _____
_____
_____

20__ _____
_____
_____

20__ _____
_____
_____

20__ _____
_____
_____

20__ _____
_____
_____

JUNE 2

20__ _____

_____

_____

20__ _____

_____

_____

20__ _____

_____

_____

20__ _____

_____

_____

20__ _____

_____

_____

20__ _____

_____

_____

JUNE 3

20__ _____

_____

_____

20__ _____

_____

_____

20__ _____

_____

_____

20__ _____

_____

_____

20__ _____

_____

_____

20__ _____

_____

_____

JUNE 4

20__ _____
_____
_____

20__ _____
_____
_____

20__ _____
_____
_____

20__ _____
_____
_____

20__ _____
_____
_____

20__ _____
_____
_____

JUNE 5

20__ _____

_____

_____

20__ _____

_____

_____

20__ _____

_____

_____

20__ _____

_____

_____

20__ _____

_____

_____

20__ _____

_____

_____

JUNE 6

20___ _____
_____
_____

20___ _____
_____
_____

20___ _____
_____
_____

20___ _____
_____
_____

20___ _____
_____
_____

20___ _____
_____
_____

JUNE 7

20__ _____

_____

_____

20__ _____

_____

_____

20__ _____

_____

_____

20__ _____

_____

_____

20__ _____

_____

_____

20__ _____

_____

_____

JUNE 8

20___ _____

_____

20___ _____

_____

20___ _____

_____

20___ _____

_____

20___ _____

_____

20___ _____

_____

JUNE 9

20___ _____

_____

20___ _____

_____

20___ _____

_____

20___ _____

_____

20___ _____

_____

20___ _____

_____

JUNE 10

20___ _____

_____

_____

20___ _____

_____

_____

20___ _____

_____

_____

20___ _____

_____

_____

20___ _____

_____

_____

20___ _____

_____

_____

JUNE 11

20___ _____

_____

_____

20___ _____

_____

_____

20___ _____

_____

_____

20___ _____

_____

_____

20___ _____

_____

_____

20___ _____

_____

_____

JUNE 12

20__ _____

_____

_____

20__ _____

_____

_____

20__ _____

_____

_____

20__ _____

_____

_____

20__ _____

_____

_____

20__ _____

_____

_____

JUNE 13

20__ _____

_____

_____

20__ _____

_____

_____

20__ _____

_____

_____

20__ _____

_____

_____

20__ _____

_____

_____

20__ _____

_____

_____

JUNE 14

20__ _____

_____

_____

20__ _____

_____

_____

20__ _____

_____

_____

20__ _____

_____

_____

20__ _____

_____

_____

20__ _____

_____

_____

JUNE 15

20___ _____

_____

_____

20___ _____

_____

_____

20___ _____

_____

_____

20___ _____

_____

_____

20___ _____

_____

_____

20___ _____

_____

_____

JUNE 16

20__ _____

_____

_____

20__ _____

_____

_____

20__ _____

_____

_____

20__ _____

_____

_____

20__ _____

_____

_____

20__ _____

_____

_____

JUNE 17

20__ _____

_____

20__ _____

_____

20__ _____

_____

20__ _____

_____

20__ _____

_____

20__ _____

_____

JUNE 18

20__ _____

_____

_____

20__ _____

_____

_____

20__ _____

_____

_____

20__ _____

_____

_____

20__ _____

_____

_____

20__ _____

_____

_____

JUNE 19

20__ _____
_____
_____

20__ _____
_____
_____

20__ _____
_____
_____

20__ _____
_____
_____

20__ _____
_____
_____

20__ _____
_____
_____

JUNE 20

20__ _____

_____

_____

20__ _____

_____

_____

20__ _____

_____

_____

20__ _____

_____

_____

20__ _____

_____

_____

20__ _____

_____

_____

JUNE 21

20__ _____

_____

_____

20__ _____

_____

_____

20__ _____

_____

_____

20__ _____

_____

_____

20__ _____

_____

_____

20__ _____

_____

_____

JUNE 22

20__ _____

_____

_____

20__ _____

_____

_____

20__ _____

_____

_____

20__ _____

_____

_____

20__ _____

_____

_____

20__ _____

_____

_____

JUNE 23

20__ _____

_____

20__ _____

_____

20__ _____

_____

20__ _____

_____

20__ _____

_____

20__ _____

_____

JUNE 24

20__ _____

_____

_____

20__ _____

_____

_____

20__ _____

_____

_____

20__ _____

_____

_____

20__ _____

_____

_____

20__ _____

_____

_____

JUNE 25

20___ _____

_____

_____

20___ _____

_____

_____

20___ _____

_____

_____

20___ _____

_____

_____

20___ _____

_____

_____

20___ _____

_____

_____

JUNE 26

20___ _____
_____
_____

20___ _____
_____
_____

20___ _____
_____
_____

20___ _____
_____
_____

20___ _____
_____
_____

20___ _____
_____
_____

JUNE 27

20__ _____

_____

_____

20__ _____

_____

_____

20__ _____

_____

_____

20__ _____

_____

_____

20__ _____

_____

_____

20__ _____

_____

_____

JUNE 28

20__ _____

_____

_____

20__ _____

_____

_____

20__ _____

_____

_____

20__ _____

_____

_____

20__ _____

_____

_____

20__ _____

_____

_____

JUNE 29

20__ _____
_____

20__ _____
_____

20__ _____
_____

20__ _____
_____

20__ _____
_____

20__ _____
_____

JUNE 30

20__ _____

_____

_____

20__ _____

_____

_____

20__ _____

_____

_____

20__ _____

_____

_____

20__ _____

_____

_____

20__ _____

_____

_____

DATES TO REMEMBER

GOALS FOR JULY

20_ 1. _____

2. _____

20_ 1. _____

2. _____

20_ 1. _____

2. _____

20_ 1. _____

2. _____

20_ 1. _____

2. _____

20_ 1. _____

2. _____

JULY 1

20__ _____
_____
_____

20__ _____
_____
_____

20__ _____
_____
_____

20__ _____
_____
_____

20__ _____
_____
_____

20__ _____
_____
_____

JULY 2

20__ _____

_____

_____

20__ _____

_____

_____

20__ _____

_____

_____

20__ _____

_____

_____

20__ _____

_____

_____

20__ _____

_____

_____

JULY 3

20__ _____

_____

20__ _____

_____

20__ _____

_____

20__ _____

_____

20__ _____

_____

20__ _____

_____

JULY 4

20___ _____

_____

_____

20___ _____

_____

_____

20___ _____

_____

_____

20___ _____

_____

_____

20___ _____

_____

_____

20___ _____

_____

_____

JULY 5

20___ _____
_____
_____

20___ _____
_____
_____

20___ _____
_____
_____

20___ _____
_____
_____

20___ _____
_____
_____

20___ _____
_____
_____

JULY 6

20___ _____

_____

_____

20___ _____

_____

_____

20___ _____

_____

_____

20___ _____

_____

_____

20___ _____

_____

_____

20___ _____

_____

_____

JULY 7

20__ _____

_____

20__ _____

_____

20__ _____

_____

20__ _____

_____

20__ _____

_____

20__ _____

_____

JULY 8

20__ _____

_____

_____

20__ _____

_____

_____

20__ _____

_____

_____

20__ _____

_____

_____

20__ _____

_____

_____

20__ _____

_____

_____

JULY 9

20___ ------------------------------

_____

20___ ------------------------------

_____

20___ ------------------------------

_____

20___ ------------------------------

_____

20___ ------------------------------

_____

20___ ------------------------------

_____

JULY 10

20__ _____
_____
_____

20__ _____
_____
_____

20__ _____
_____
_____

20__ _____
_____
_____

20__ _____
_____
_____

20__ _____
_____
_____

JULY 11

20__ _____

_____

_____

20__ _____

_____

_____

20__ _____

_____

_____

20__ _____

_____

_____

20__ _____

_____

_____

20__ _____

_____

_____

JULY 12

20__ _____

_____

_____

20__ _____

_____

_____

20__ _____

_____

_____

20__ _____

_____

_____

20__ _____

_____

_____

20__ _____

_____

_____

JULY 13

20___ _____
_____
_____

20___ _____
_____
_____

20___ _____
_____
_____

20___ _____
_____
_____

20___ _____
_____
_____

20___ _____
_____
_____

JULY 14

20__ _____

_____

_____

20__ _____

_____

_____

20__ _____

_____

_____

20__ _____

_____

_____

20__ _____

_____

_____

20__ _____

_____

_____

JULY 15

20__ _____

_____

_____

20__ _____

_____

_____

20__ _____

_____

_____

20__ _____

_____

_____

20__ _____

_____

_____

20__ _____

_____

_____

JULY 16

20__ _____
_____
_____

20__ _____
_____
_____

20__ _____
_____
_____

20__ _____
_____
_____

20__ _____
_____
_____

20__ _____
_____
_____

JULY 17

20__ _____

_____

20__ _____

_____

20__ _____

_____

20__ _____

_____

20__ _____

_____

20__ _____

_____

JULY 18

20__ _____

_____

_____

20__ _____

_____

_____

20__ _____

_____

_____

20__ _____

_____

_____

20__ _____

_____

_____

20__ _____

_____

_____

JULY 19

20__ _____

_____

_____

20__ _____

_____

_____

20__ _____

_____

_____

20__ _____

_____

_____

20__ _____

_____

_____

20__ _____

_____

_____

JULY 20

20___ _____

_____

_____

20___ _____

_____

_____

20___ _____

_____

_____

20___ _____

_____

_____

20___ _____

_____

_____

20___ _____

_____

_____

JULY 21

20___ _____

_____

_____

20___ _____

_____

_____

20___ _____

_____

_____

20___ _____

_____

_____

20___ _____

_____

_____

20___ _____

_____

_____

JULY 22

20___ _____

_____

_____

20___ _____

_____

_____

20___ _____

_____

_____

20___ _____

_____

_____

20___ _____

_____

_____

20___ _____

_____

_____

JULY 23

20__ _____

_____

_____

20__ _____

_____

_____

20__ _____

_____

_____

20__ _____

_____

_____

20__ _____

_____

_____

20__ _____

_____

_____

JULY 24

20__ _____

_____

_____

20__ _____

_____

_____

20__ _____

_____

_____

20__ _____

_____

_____

20__ _____

_____

_____

20__ _____

_____

_____

JULY 25

20___ _____

_____

_____

20___ _____

_____

_____

20___ _____

_____

_____

20___ _____

_____

_____

20___ _____

_____

_____

20___ _____

_____

_____

JULY 26

20__ _____

_____

_____

20__ _____

_____

_____

20__ _____

_____

_____

20__ _____

_____

_____

20__ _____

_____

_____

20__ _____

_____

_____

JULY 27

20__ _____

_____

_____

20__ _____

_____

_____

20__ _____

_____

_____

20__ _____

_____

_____

20__ _____

_____

_____

20__ _____

_____

_____

JULY 28

20__ _____

_____

20__ _____

_____

20__ _____

_____

20__ _____

_____

20__ _____

_____

20__ _____

_____

JULY 29

20__ _____

_____

_____

20__ _____

_____

_____

20__ _____

_____

_____

20__ _____

_____

_____

20__ _____

_____

_____

20__ _____

_____

_____

JULY 30

20___ _____

_____

_____

20___ _____

_____

_____

20___ _____

_____

_____

20___ _____

_____

_____

20___ _____

_____

_____

20___ _____

_____

_____

JULY 31

20__ _____

_____

_____

20__ _____

_____

_____

20__ _____

_____

_____

20__ _____

_____

_____

20__ _____

_____

_____

20__ _____

_____

_____

DATES TO REMEMBER

GOALS FOR AUGUST

20_ 1. _____

2. _____

20_ 1. _____

2. _____

20_ 1. _____

2. _____

20_ 1. _____

2. _____

20_ 1. _____

2. _____

20_ 1. _____

2. _____

AUGUST 1

20___ _____
_____
_____

20___ _____
_____
_____

20___ _____
_____
_____

20___ _____
_____
_____

20___ _____
_____
_____

20___ _____
_____
_____

AUGUST 2

20__ _____

_____

_____

20__ _____

_____

_____

20__ _____

_____

_____

20__ _____

_____

_____

20__ _____

_____

_____

20__ _____

_____

_____

AUGUST 3

20__ _____

_____

_____

20__ _____

_____

_____

20__ _____

_____

_____

20__ _____

_____

_____

20__ _____

_____

_____

20__ _____

_____

_____

AUGUST 4

20__ _____

_____

_____

20__ _____

_____

_____

20__ _____

_____

_____

20__ _____

_____

_____

20__ _____

_____

_____

20__ _____

_____

_____

AUGUST 5

20__ _____

_____

_____

20__ _____

_____

_____

20__ _____

_____

_____

20__ _____

_____

_____

20__ _____

_____

_____

20__ _____

_____

_____

AUGUST 6

20___ _____

_____

_____

20___ _____

_____

_____

20___ _____

_____

_____

20___ _____

_____

_____

20___ _____

_____

_____

20___ _____

_____

_____

AUGUST 7

20__ _____

_____

_____

20__ _____

_____

_____

20__ _____

_____

_____

20__ _____

_____

_____

20__ _____

_____

_____

20__ _____

_____

_____

AUGUST 8

20__ _____

_____

_____

20__ _____

_____

_____

20__ _____

_____

_____

20__ _____

_____

_____

20__ _____

_____

_____

20__ _____

_____

_____

AUGUST 9

20__ _____

_____

_____

20__ _____

_____

_____

20__ _____

_____

_____

20__ _____

_____

_____

20__ _____

_____

_____

20__ _____

_____

_____

AUGUST 10

20__ _____

_____

20__ _____

_____

20__ _____

_____

20__ _____

_____

20__ _____

_____

20__ _____

_____

AUGUST 11

20__ _____
_____
_____

20__ _____
_____
_____

20__ _____
_____
_____

20__ _____
_____
_____

20__ _____
_____
_____

20__ _____
_____
_____

AUGUST 12

20__ _____

_____

_____

20__ _____

_____

_____

20__ _____

_____

_____

20__ _____

_____

_____

20__ _____

_____

_____

20__ _____

_____

_____

AUGUST 13

20__ _____

_____

_____

20__ _____

_____

_____

20__ _____

_____

_____

20__ _____

_____

_____

20__ _____

_____

_____

20__ _____

_____

_____

AUGUST 14

20__ _____

_____

_____

20__ _____

_____

_____

20__ _____

_____

_____

20__ _____

_____

_____

20__ _____

_____

_____

20__ _____

_____

_____

AUGUST 15

20__ _____

_____

20__ _____

_____

20__ _____

_____

20__ _____

_____

20__ _____

_____

20__ _____

_____

AUGUST 16

20__ _____

_____

_____

20__ _____

_____

_____

20__ _____

_____

_____

20__ _____

_____

_____

20__ _____

_____

_____

20__ _____

_____

_____

AUGUST 17

20__ _____

_____

_____

20__ _____

_____

_____

20__ _____

_____

_____

20__ _____

_____

_____

20__ _____

_____

_____

20__ _____

_____

_____

AUGUST 18

20___ _____

_____

_____

20___ _____

_____

_____

20___ _____

_____

_____

20___ _____

_____

_____

20___ _____

_____

_____

20___ _____

_____

_____

AUGUST 19

20__ _____

_____

_____

20__ _____

_____

_____

20__ _____

_____

_____

20__ _____

_____

_____

20__ _____

_____

_____

20__ _____

_____

_____

AUGUST 20

20___ _____

_____

_____

20___ _____

_____

_____

20___ _____

_____

_____

20___ _____

_____

_____

20___ _____

_____

_____

20___ _____

_____

_____

AUGUST 21

20___ _____

_____

_____

20___ _____

_____

_____

20___ _____

_____

_____

20___ _____

_____

_____

20___ _____

_____

_____

20___ _____

_____

_____

AUGUST 22

20__ _____

_____

_____

20__ _____

_____

_____

20__ _____

_____

_____

20__ _____

_____

_____

20__ _____

_____

_____

20__ _____

_____

_____

AUGUST 23

20___ _____

_____

_____

20___ _____

_____

_____

20___ _____

_____

_____

20___ _____

_____

_____

20___ _____

_____

_____

20___ _____

_____

_____

AUGUST 24

20__ _____

_____

_____

20__ _____

_____

_____

20__ _____

_____

_____

20__ _____

_____

_____

20__ _____

_____

_____

20__ _____

_____

_____

AUGUST 25

20__ _____

_____

_____

20__ _____

_____

_____

20__ _____

_____

_____

20__ _____

_____

_____

20__ _____

_____

_____

20__ _____

_____

_____

AUGUST 26

20__ _____

_____

_____

20__ _____

_____

_____

20__ _____

_____

_____

20__ _____

_____

_____

20__ _____

_____

_____

20__ _____

_____

_____

AUGUST 27

20__ _____

_____

_____

20__ _____

_____

_____

20__ _____

_____

_____

20__ _____

_____

_____

20__ _____

_____

_____

20__ _____

_____

_____

AUGUST 28

20__ _____

_____

_____

20__ _____

_____

_____

20__ _____

_____

_____

20__ _____

_____

_____

20__ _____

_____

_____

20__ _____

_____

_____

AUGUST 29

20__ _____

_____

_____

20__ _____

_____

_____

20__ _____

_____

_____

20__ _____

_____

_____

20__ _____

_____

_____

20__ _____

_____

_____

AUGUST 30

20__ _____

_____

_____

20__ _____

_____

_____

20__ _____

_____

_____

20__ _____

_____

_____

20__ _____

_____

_____

20__ _____

_____

_____

AUGUST 31

20__ _____

_____

_____

20__ _____

_____

_____

20__ _____

_____

_____

20__ _____

_____

_____

20__ _____

_____

_____

20__ _____

_____

_____

DATES TO REMEMBER

GOALS FOR SEPTEMBER

20_ 1. _____

2. _____

20_ 1. _____

2. _____

20_ 1. _____

2. _____

20_ 1. _____

2. _____

20_ 1. _____

2. _____

20_ 1. _____

2. _____

SEPTEMBER 1

20__ _____

_____

_____

20__ _____

_____

_____

20__ _____

_____

_____

20__ _____

_____

_____

20__ _____

_____

_____

20__ _____

_____

_____

SEPTEMBER 2

20__ _____

_____

_____

20__ _____

_____

_____

20__ _____

_____

_____

20__ _____

_____

_____

20__ _____

_____

_____

20__ _____

_____

_____

SEPTEMBER 3

20__ _____

_____

_____

20__ _____

_____

_____

20__ _____

_____

_____

20__ _____

_____

_____

20__ _____

_____

_____

20__ _____

_____

_____

SEPTEMBER 4

20__ _____

_____

_____

20__ _____

_____

_____

20__ _____

_____

_____

20__ _____

_____

_____

20__ _____

_____

_____

20__ _____

_____

_____

SEPTEMBER 5

20__ _____

_____

_____

20__ _____

_____

_____

20__ _____

_____

_____

20__ _____

_____

_____

20__ _____

_____

_____

20__ _____

_____

_____

SEPTEMBER 6

20___ _____

_____

_____

20___ _____

_____

_____

20___ _____

_____

_____

20___ _____

_____

_____

20___ _____

_____

_____

20___ _____

_____

_____

SEPTEMBER 7

20___ _____

_____

_____

20___ _____

_____

_____

20___ _____

_____

_____

20___ _____

_____

_____

20___ _____

_____

_____

20___ _____

_____

_____

SEPTEMBER 8

20___ _____

_____

_____

20___ _____

_____

_____

20___ _____

_____

_____

20___ _____

_____

_____

20___ _____

_____

_____

20___ _____

_____

_____

SEPTEMBER 9

20__ _____

_____

_____

20__ _____

_____

_____

20__ _____

_____

_____

20__ _____

_____

_____

20__ _____

_____

_____

20__ _____

_____

_____

SEPTEMBER 10

20__ _____

_____

_____

20__ _____

_____

_____

20__ _____

_____

_____

20__ _____

_____

_____

20__ _____

_____

_____

20__ _____

_____

_____

SEPTEMBER 11

20__ _____

_____

_____

20__ _____

_____

_____

20__ _____

_____

_____

20__ _____

_____

_____

20__ _____

_____

_____

20__ _____

_____

_____

SEPTEMBER 12

20__ _____

_____

_____

20__ _____

_____

_____

20__ _____

_____

_____

20__ _____

_____

_____

20__ _____

_____

_____

20__ _____

_____

_____

SEPTEMBER 13

20__ _____

_____

_____

20__ _____

_____

_____

20__ _____

_____

_____

20__ _____

_____

_____

20__ _____

_____

_____

20__ _____

_____

_____

SEPTEMBER 14

20___ _____

_____

_____

20___ _____

_____

_____

20___ _____

_____

_____

20___ _____

_____

_____

20___ _____

_____

_____

20___ _____

_____

_____

SEPTEMBER 15

20__ _____

_____

_____

20__ _____

_____

_____

20__ _____

_____

_____

20__ _____

_____

_____

20__ _____

_____

_____

20__ _____

_____

_____

SEPTEMBER 16

20__ _____

_____

_____

20__ _____

_____

_____

20__ _____

_____

_____

20__ _____

_____

_____

20__ _____

_____

_____

20__ _____

_____

_____

SEPTEMBER 17

20__ _____

_____

_____

20__ _____

_____

_____

20__ _____

_____

_____

20__ _____

_____

_____

20__ _____

_____

_____

20__ _____

_____

_____

SEPTEMBER 18

20__ _____

_____

_____

20__ _____

_____

_____

20__ _____

_____

_____

20__ _____

_____

_____

20__ _____

_____

_____

20__ _____

_____

_____

SEPTEMBER 19

20__ _____

_____

_____

20__ _____

_____

_____

20__ _____

_____

_____

20__ _____

_____

_____

20__ _____

_____

_____

20__ _____

_____

_____

SEPTEMBER 20

20__ _____

_____

_____

20__ _____

_____

_____

20__ _____

_____

_____

20__ _____

_____

_____

20__ _____

_____

_____

20__ _____

_____

_____

SEPTEMBER 21

20__ _____
_____
_____

20__ _____
_____
_____

20__ _____
_____
_____

20__ _____
_____
_____

20__ _____
_____
_____

20__ _____
_____
_____

SEPTEMBER 22

20___ _____

_____

_____

20___ _____

_____

_____

20___ _____

_____

_____

20___ _____

_____

_____

20___ _____

_____

_____

20___ _____

_____

_____

SEPTEMBER 23

20___ _____
_____
_____

20___ _____
_____
_____

20___ _____
_____
_____

20___ _____
_____
_____

20___ _____
_____
_____

20___ _____
_____
_____

SEPTEMBER 24

20__ _____

_____

_____

20__ _____

_____

_____

20__ _____

_____

_____

20__ _____

_____

_____

20__ _____

_____

_____

20__ _____

_____

_____

SEPTEMBER 25

20__ _____

_____

_____

20__ _____

_____

_____

20__ _____

_____

_____

20__ _____

_____

_____

20__ _____

_____

_____

20__ _____

_____

_____

SEPTEMBER 26

20__ _____

_____

_____

20__ _____

_____

_____

20__ _____

_____

_____

20__ _____

_____

_____

20__ _____

_____

_____

20__ _____

_____

_____

SEPTEMBER 27

20__ _____

_____

20__ _____

_____

20__ _____

_____

20__ _____

_____

20__ _____

_____

20__ _____

_____

SEPTEMBER 28

20__ _____

_____

_____

20__ _____

_____

_____

20__ _____

_____

_____

20__ _____

_____

_____

20__ _____

_____

_____

20__ _____

_____

_____

SEPTEMBER 29

20__ _____

_____

_____

20__ _____

_____

_____

20__ _____

_____

_____

20__ _____

_____

_____

20__ _____

_____

_____

20__ _____

_____

_____

SEPTEMBER 30

20__ _____

_____

_____

20__ _____

_____

_____

20__ _____

_____

_____

20__ _____

_____

_____

20__ _____

_____

_____

20__ _____

_____

_____

DATES TO REMEMBER

GOALS FOR OCTOBER

20_ 1. _____

2. _____

20_ 1. _____

2. _____

20_ 1. _____

2. _____

20_ 1. _____

2. _____

20_ 1. _____

2. _____

20_ 1. _____

2. _____

OCTOBER 1

20__ ------------------------------

_____

20__ ------------------------------

_____

20__ ------------------------------

_____

20__ ------------------------------

_____

20__ ------------------------------

_____

20__ ------------------------------

_____

OCTOBER 2

20__ _____

_____

_____

20__ _____

_____

_____

20__ _____

_____

_____

20__ _____

_____

_____

20__ _____

_____

_____

20__ _____

_____

_____

OCTOBER 3

20___ _____

_____

_____

20___ _____

_____

_____

20___ _____

_____

_____

20___ _____

_____

_____

20___ _____

_____

_____

20___ _____

_____

_____

OCTOBER 4

20__ _____

_____

_____

20__ _____

_____

_____

20__ _____

_____

_____

20__ _____

_____

_____

20__ _____

_____

_____

20__ _____

_____

_____

OCTOBER 5

20__ _____
_____
_____

20__ _____
_____
_____

20__ _____
_____
_____

20__ _____
_____
_____

20__ _____
_____
_____

20__ _____
_____
_____

OCTOBER 6

20__ _____

_____

_____

20__ _____

_____

_____

20__ _____

_____

_____

20__ _____

_____

_____

20__ _____

_____

_____

20__ _____

_____

_____

OCTOBER 7

20__ _____
_____
_____

20__ _____
_____
_____

20__ _____
_____
_____

20__ _____
_____
_____

20__ _____
_____
_____

20__ _____
_____
_____

OCTOBER 8

20__ _____

_____

_____

20__ _____

_____

_____

20__ _____

_____

_____

20__ _____

_____

_____

20__ _____

_____

_____

20__ _____

_____

_____

OCTOBER 9

20__ _____
_____
_____

20__ _____
_____
_____

20__ _____
_____
_____

20__ _____
_____
_____

20__ _____
_____
_____

20__ _____
_____
_____

OCTOBER 10

20__ _____

_____

_____

20__ _____

_____

_____

20__ _____

_____

_____

20__ _____

_____

_____

20__ _____

_____

_____

20__ _____

_____

_____

OCTOBER 11

20___ _____
_____
_____

20___ _____
_____
_____

20___ _____
_____
_____

20___ _____
_____
_____

20___ _____
_____
_____

20___ _____
_____
_____

OCTOBER 12

20__ _____

_____

_____

20__ _____

_____

_____

20__ _____

_____

_____

20__ _____

_____

_____

20__ _____

_____

_____

20__ _____

_____

_____

OCTOBER 13

20__ _____
_____
_____

20__ _____
_____
_____

20__ _____
_____
_____

20__ _____
_____
_____

20__ _____
_____
_____

20__ _____
_____
_____

OCTOBER 14

20__ _____

_____

_____

20__ _____

_____

_____

20__ _____

_____

_____

20__ _____

_____

_____

20__ _____

_____

_____

20__ _____

_____

_____

OCTOBER 15

20__ _____

_____

_____

20__ _____

_____

_____

20__ _____

_____

_____

20__ _____

_____

_____

20__ _____

_____

_____

20__ _____

_____

_____

OCTOBER 16

20__ _____

_____

_____

20__ _____

_____

_____

20__ _____

_____

_____

20__ _____

_____

_____

20__ _____

_____

_____

20__ _____

_____

_____

OCTOBER 17

20___ _____

_____

_____

20___ _____

_____

_____

20___ _____

_____

_____

20___ _____

_____

_____

20___ _____

_____

_____

20___ _____

_____

_____

OCTOBER 18

20__ _____
_____
_____

20__ _____
_____
_____

20__ _____
_____
_____

20__ _____
_____
_____

20__ _____
_____
_____

20__ _____
_____
_____

OCTOBER 19

20__ _____

_____

_____

20__ _____

_____

_____

20__ _____

_____

_____

20__ _____

_____

_____

20__ _____

_____

_____

20__ _____

_____

_____

OCTOBER 20

20___ _____

_____

_____

20___ _____

_____

_____

20___ _____

_____

_____

20___ _____

_____

_____

20___ _____

_____

_____

20___ _____

_____

_____

OCTOBER 21

20__ _____

_____

_____

20__ _____

_____

_____

20__ _____

_____

_____

20__ _____

_____

_____

20__ _____

_____

_____

20__ _____

_____

_____

OCTOBER 22

20__ _____

_____

_____

20__ _____

_____

_____

20__ _____

_____

_____

20__ _____

_____

_____

20__ _____

_____

_____

20__ _____

_____

_____

OCTOBER 23

20__ _____

_____

_____

20__ _____

_____

_____

20__ _____

_____

_____

20__ _____

_____

_____

20__ _____

_____

_____

20__ _____

_____

_____

OCTOBER 24

20__ _____

_____

_____

20__ _____

_____

_____

20__ _____

_____

_____

20__ _____

_____

_____

20__ _____

_____

_____

20__ _____

_____

_____

OCTOBER 25

20__ _____

_____

_____

20__ _____

_____

_____

20__ _____

_____

_____

20__ _____

_____

_____

20__ _____

_____

_____

20__ _____

_____

_____

OCTOBER 26

20___ _____

_____

_____

20___ _____

_____

_____

20___ _____

_____

_____

20___ _____

_____

_____

20___ _____

_____

_____

20___ _____

_____

_____

OCTOBER 27

20__ _____

_____

_____

20__ _____

_____

_____

20__ _____

_____

_____

20__ _____

_____

_____

20__ _____

_____

_____

20__ _____

_____

_____

OCTOBER 28

20__ _____

_____

_____

20__ _____

_____

_____

20__ _____

_____

_____

20__ _____

_____

_____

20__ _____

_____

_____

20__ _____

_____

_____

OCTOBER 29

20___ _____

_____

_____

20___ _____

_____

_____

20___ _____

_____

_____

20___ _____

_____

_____

20___ _____

_____

_____

20___ _____

_____

_____

OCTOBER 30

20__ _____

_____

_____

20__ _____

_____

_____

20__ _____

_____

_____

20__ _____

_____

_____

20__ _____

_____

_____

20__ _____

_____

_____

OCTOBER 31

20__ _____

_____

_____

20__ _____

_____

_____

20__ _____

_____

_____

20__ _____

_____

_____

20__ _____

_____

_____

20__ _____

_____

_____

DATES TO REMEMBER

_____

_____

_____

_____

_____

_____

_____

_____

_____

_____

_____

_____

_____

_____

_____

_____

_____

GOALS FOR NOVEMBER

20_ 1. _____

2. _____

20_ 1. _____

2. _____

20_ 1. _____

2. _____

20_ 1. _____

2. _____

20_ 1. _____

2. _____

20_ 1. _____

2. _____

NOVEMBER 1

20__ _____

_____

_____

20__ _____

_____

_____

20__ _____

_____

_____

20__ _____

_____

_____

20__ _____

_____

_____

20__ _____

_____

_____

NOVEMBER 2

20__ _____

_____

_____

20__ _____

_____

_____

20__ _____

_____

_____

20__ _____

_____

_____

20__ _____

_____

_____

20__ _____

_____

_____

NOVEMBER 3

20__ _____

_____

_____

20__ _____

_____

_____

20__ _____

_____

_____

20__ _____

_____

_____

20__ _____

_____

_____

20__ _____

_____

_____

NOVEMBER 4

20___ _____

_____

_____

20___ _____

_____

_____

20___ _____

_____

_____

20___ _____

_____

_____

20___ _____

_____

_____

20___ _____

_____

_____

NOVEMBER 5

20__ _____

_____

_____

20__ _____

_____

_____

20__ _____

_____

_____

20__ _____

_____

_____

20__ _____

_____

_____

20__ _____

_____

_____

NOVEMBER 6

20__ _____

_____

_____

20__ _____

_____

_____

20__ _____

_____

_____

20__ _____

_____

_____

20__ _____

_____

_____

20__ _____

_____

_____

NOVEMBER 6

20__ _____

_____

_____

20__ _____

_____

_____

20__ _____

_____

_____

20__ _____

_____

_____

20__ _____

_____

_____

20__ _____

_____

_____

NOVEMBER 7

20___ _____
_____
_____

20___ _____
_____
_____

20___ _____
_____
_____

20___ _____
_____
_____

20___ _____
_____
_____

20___ _____
_____
_____

NOVEMBER 8

20__ _____

_____

_____

20__ _____

_____

_____

20__ _____

_____

_____

20__ _____

_____

_____

20__ _____

_____

_____

20__ _____

_____

_____

NOVEMBER 9

20__ _____

_____

_____

20__ _____

_____

_____

20__ _____

_____

_____

20__ _____

_____

_____

20__ _____

_____

_____

20__ _____

_____

_____

NOVEMBER 10

20__ _____

_____

_____

20__ _____

_____

_____

20__ _____

_____

_____

20__ _____

_____

_____

20__ _____

_____

_____

20__ _____

_____

_____

NOVEMBER 11

20__ _____

_____

_____

20__ _____

_____

_____

20__ _____

_____

_____

20__ _____

_____

_____

20__ _____

_____

_____

20__ _____

_____

_____

NOVEMBER 12

20__ _____

_____

_____

20__ _____

_____

_____

20__ _____

_____

_____

20__ _____

_____

_____

20__ _____

_____

_____

20__ _____

_____

_____

NOVEMBER 13

20__ _____

_____

_____

20__ _____

_____

_____

20__ _____

_____

_____

20__ _____

_____

_____

20__ _____

_____

_____

20__ _____

_____

_____

NOVEMBER 14

20___ _____

_____

_____

20___ _____

_____

_____

20___ _____

_____

_____

20___ _____

_____

_____

20___ _____

_____

_____

20___ _____

_____

_____

NOVEMBER 15

20__ _____

_____

_____

20__ _____

_____

_____

20__ _____

_____

_____

20__ _____

_____

_____

20__ _____

_____

_____

20__ _____

_____

_____

NOVEMBER 16

20__ _____

_____

_____

20__ _____

_____

_____

20__ _____

_____

_____

20__ _____

_____

_____

20__ _____

_____

_____

20__ _____

_____

_____

NOVEMBER 17

20__ _____

_____

_____

20__ _____

_____

_____

20__ _____

_____

_____

20__ _____

_____

_____

20__ _____

_____

_____

20__ _____

_____

_____

NOVEMBER 18

20__ _____

_____

_____

20__ _____

_____

_____

20__ _____

_____

_____

20__ _____

_____

_____

20__ _____

_____

_____

20__ _____

_____

_____

NOVEMBER 19

20__ _____

_____

_____

20__ _____

_____

_____

20__ _____

_____

_____

20__ _____

_____

_____

20__ _____

_____

_____

20__ _____

_____

_____

NOVEMBER 20

20__ _____

_____

_____

20__ _____

_____

_____

20__ _____

_____

_____

20__ _____

_____

_____

20__ _____

_____

_____

20__ _____

_____

_____

NOVEMBER 21

20___ _____

_____

_____

20___ _____

_____

_____

20___ _____

_____

_____

20___ _____

_____

_____

20___ _____

_____

_____

20___ _____

_____

_____

NOVEMBER 22

20___ _____

_____

_____

20___ _____

_____

_____

20___ _____

_____

_____

20___ _____

_____

_____

20___ _____

_____

_____

20___ _____

_____

_____

NOVEMBER 23

20___ _____

_____

_____

20___ _____

_____

_____

20___ _____

_____

_____

20___ _____

_____

_____

20___ _____

_____

_____

20___ _____

_____

_____

NOVEMBER 24

20__ _____

_____

_____

20__ _____

_____

_____

20__ _____

_____

_____

20__ _____

_____

_____

20__ _____

_____

_____

20__ _____

_____

_____

NOVEMBER 25

20__ _____

_____

_____

20__ _____

_____

_____

20__ _____

_____

_____

20__ _____

_____

_____

20__ _____

_____

_____

20__ _____

_____

_____

NOVEMBER 26

20__ _____

_____

_____

20__ _____

_____

_____

20__ _____

_____

_____

20__ _____

_____

_____

20__ _____

_____

_____

20__ _____

_____

_____

NOVEMBER 27

20__ _____

_____

_____

20__ _____

_____

_____

20__ _____

_____

_____

20__ _____

_____

_____

20__ _____

_____

_____

20__ _____

_____

_____

NOVEMBER 28

20__ _____

_____

_____

20__ _____

_____

_____

20__ _____

_____

_____

20__ _____

_____

_____

20__ _____

_____

_____

20__ _____

_____

_____

NOVEMBER 29

20__ _____

_____

_____

20__ _____

_____

_____

20__ _____

_____

_____

20__ _____

_____

_____

20__ _____

_____

_____

20__ _____

_____

_____

NOVEMBER 30

20__ _____

_____

_____

20__ _____

_____

_____

20__ _____

_____

_____

20__ _____

_____

_____

20__ _____

_____

_____

20__ _____

_____

_____

DATES TO REMEMBER

GOALS FOR DECEMBER

20_ 1. _____

2. _____

20_ 1. _____

2. _____

20_ 1. _____

2. _____

20_ 1. _____

2. _____

20_ 1. _____

2. _____

20_ 1. _____

2. _____

DECEMBER 1

20___ _____

_____

_____

20___ _____

_____

_____

20___ _____

_____

_____

20___ _____

_____

_____

20___ _____

_____

_____

20___ _____

_____

_____

DECEMBER 2

20__ _____

_____

_____

20__ _____

_____

_____

20__ _____

_____

_____

20__ _____

_____

_____

20__ _____

_____

_____

20__ _____

_____

_____

DECEMBER 3

20___ _____

_____

_____

20___ _____

_____

_____

20___ _____

_____

_____

20___ _____

_____

_____

20___ _____

_____

_____

20___ _____

_____

_____

DECEMBER 4

20__ _____

_____

_____

20__ _____

_____

_____

20__ _____

_____

_____

20__ _____

_____

_____

20__ _____

_____

_____

20__ _____

_____

_____

DECEMBER 5

20__ _____

_____

20__ _____

_____

20__ _____

_____

20__ _____

_____

20__ _____

_____

20__ _____

_____

DECEMBER 6

20___ _____

_____

_____

20___ _____

_____

_____

20___ _____

_____

_____

20___ _____

_____

_____

20___ _____

_____

_____

20___ _____

_____

_____

DECEMBER 7

20__ _____
_____
_____

20__ _____
_____
_____

20__ _____
_____
_____

20__ _____
_____
_____

20__ _____
_____
_____

20__ _____
_____
_____

DECEMBER 8

20___ _____

_____

_____

20___ _____

_____

_____

20___ _____

_____

_____

20___ _____

_____

_____

20___ _____

_____

_____

20___ _____

_____

_____

DECEMBER 9

20__ _____

_____

_____

20__ _____

_____

_____

20__ _____

_____

_____

20__ _____

_____

_____

20__ _____

_____

_____

20__ _____

_____

_____

DECEMBER 10

20__ _____

_____

_____

20__ _____

_____

_____

20__ _____

_____

_____

20__ _____

_____

_____

20__ _____

_____

_____

20__ _____

_____

_____

DECEMBER 11

20__ _____

_____

_____

20__ _____

_____

_____

20__ _____

_____

_____

20__ _____

_____

_____

20__ _____

_____

_____

20__ _____

_____

_____

DECEMBER 12

20__ _____

_____

_____

20__ _____

_____

_____

20__ _____

_____

_____

20__ _____

_____

_____

20__ _____

_____

_____

20__ _____

_____

_____

DECEMBER 13

20___ _____
_____
_____

20___ _____
_____
_____

20___ _____
_____
_____

20___ _____
_____
_____

20___ _____
_____
_____

20___ _____
_____
_____

DECEMBER 14

20___ _____

_____

_____

20___ _____

_____

_____

20___ _____

_____

_____

20___ _____

_____

_____

20___ _____

_____

_____

20___ _____

_____

_____

DECEMBER 15

20__ _____

_____

_____

20__ _____

_____

_____

20__ _____

_____

_____

20__ _____

_____

_____

20__ _____

_____

_____

20__ _____

_____

_____

DECEMBER 16

20___ _____

_____

_____

20___ _____

_____

_____

20___ _____

_____

_____

20___ _____

_____

_____

20___ _____

_____

_____

20___ _____

_____

_____

DECEMBER 16

20__ _____

_____

_____

20__ _____

_____

_____

20__ _____

_____

_____

20__ _____

_____

_____

20__ _____

_____

_____

20__ _____

_____

_____

DECEMBER 17

20__ _____

_____

_____

20__ _____

_____

_____

20__ _____

_____

_____

20__ _____

_____

_____

20__ _____

_____

_____

20__ _____

_____

_____

DECEMBER 18

20__ _____
_____
_____

20__ _____
_____
_____

20__ _____
_____
_____

20__ _____
_____
_____

20__ _____
_____
_____

20__ _____
_____
_____

DECEMBER 19

20___ _____

_____

_____

20___ _____

_____

_____

20___ _____

_____

_____

20___ _____

_____

_____

20___ _____

_____

_____

20___ _____

_____

_____

DECEMBER 20

20___ _____

_____

_____

20___ _____

_____

_____

20___ _____

_____

_____

20___ _____

_____

_____

20___ _____

_____

_____

20___ _____

_____

_____

DECEMBER 21

20__ _____

_____

_____

20__ _____

_____

_____

20__ _____

_____

_____

20__ _____

_____

_____

20__ _____

_____

_____

20__ _____

_____

_____

DECEMBER 22

20__ _____
_____
_____

20__ _____
_____
_____

20__ _____
_____
_____

20__ _____
_____
_____

20__ _____
_____
_____

20__ _____
_____
_____

DECEMBER 23

20__ _____

_____

_____

20__ _____

_____

_____

20__ _____

_____

_____

20__ _____

_____

_____

20__ _____

_____

_____

20__ _____

_____

_____

DECEMBER 24

20__ _____

_____

_____

20__ _____

_____

_____

20__ _____

_____

_____

20__ _____

_____

_____

20__ _____

_____

_____

20__ _____

_____

_____

DECEMBER 25

20___ _____

_____

_____

20___ _____

_____

_____

20___ _____

_____

_____

20___ _____

_____

_____

20___ _____

_____

_____

20___ _____

_____

_____

DECEMBER 26

20___ _____
_____
_____

20___ _____
_____
_____

20___ _____
_____
_____

20___ _____
_____
_____

20___ _____
_____
_____

20___ _____
_____
_____

DECEMBER 27

20__ _____

_____

_____

20__ _____

_____

_____

20__ _____

_____

_____

20__ _____

_____

_____

20__ _____

_____

_____

20__ _____

_____

_____

DECEMBER 28

20___ _____
_____
_____

20___ _____
_____
_____

20___ _____
_____
_____

20___ _____
_____
_____

20___ _____
_____
_____

20___ _____
_____
_____

DECEMBER 29

20___ _____

_____

_____

20___ _____

_____

_____

20___ _____

_____

_____

20___ _____

_____

_____

20___ _____

_____

_____

20___ _____

_____

_____

DECEMBER 30

20___ _____
_____
_____

20___ _____
_____
_____

20___ _____
_____
_____

20___ _____
_____
_____

20___ _____
_____
_____

20___ _____
_____
_____

DECEMBER 31

20__ _____

_____

_____

20__ _____

_____

_____

20__ _____

_____

_____

20__ _____

_____

_____

20__ _____

_____

_____

20__ _____

_____

_____

DATES TO REMEMBER

Thank you for purchasing this journal and I hope you enjoyed it. Join Lovestories Press Facebook group to stay in the know on upcoming releases, giveaways and a better way to connect with us!

With love, Lovestories Press

CPSIA information can be obtained
at www.ICGtesting.com
Printed in the USA
LVHW021437220121
677072LV00002B/22